Anonymous

The Lincoln Catechism

Wherein the eccentricities & beauties of despotism are fully set forth. A

guide to the presidential election of 1864

Anonymous

The Lincoln Catechism
Wherein the eccentricities & beauties of despotism are fully set forth. A guide to the presidential election of 1864

ISBN/EAN: 9783337411114

Printed in Europe, USA, Canada, Australia, Japan

Cover: Foto ©Suzi / pixelio.de

More available books at **www.hansebooks.com**

THE
LINCOLN
CATECHISM

WHEREIN THE

Eccentricities & Beauties of Despotism

ARE FULLY SET FORTH.

A Guide to the Presidential Election of 1864

J. F. FEEKS, PUBLISHER,

No. 26 ANN STREET, N. Y.

THE LINCOLN

CATECHISM.

LESSON THE FIRST.

I.

What is the Constitution?

A compact with hell—now obsolete.

II.

By whom hath the Constitution been made obsolete?

By Abraham Africanus the First.

III.

To what end?

That his days may be long in office—and that he may make himself and his people the equal of the negroes.

IV.

What is a President?

A general agent for negroes.

V.

What is Congress?

A body organized for the purpose of taxing the people to buy negroes, and to make laws to protect the President from being punished for his crimes.

VI.

What is an army?

A provost guard, to arrest white men, and set negroes free.

VII.

Who are members of Congress supposed to represent?

The President and his Cabinet.

·VIII.

What is the meaning of *coining money?*

Printing green paper.

IX.

What did the Constitution mean by freedom of the Press?

Throwing Democratic newspapers out of the mails

X.

What is the meaning of the word Liberty?

Incarceration in a vermin-infested bastile.

XI.

What is the duty of a Secretary of War?

To arrest freemen by telegraph.

XII. ·

What are the duties of a Secretary of the Navy?

To build and sink gunboats.

XIII.

What is the business of a Secretary of the Treasury?

To destroy State Banks and fill the pockets of the people full of worthless, irredeemable U. S. shinplasters.

XIV.

What is the chief business of a Secretary of State?

To print five volumes a year of Foreign Correspondence with himself, to drink whisky, and prophesy about war.

XV.

What is the meaning of the word "patriot?"

A man who loves his country less, and the negro more.

XVI.

What is the meaning of the word "traitor?"

One who is a stickler for the Constitution and the laws.

XVII.

What is the meaning of the word "Copperhead?"

A man who believes in the Union as it was, the Constitution as it is, and who cannot be bribed with greenbacks, nor frightened by a bastile.

XVIII.

What is a "loyal league?"

A body of men banded together, with secret signs and pass words, for the purpose of making a negro of a white man, and of controlling elections by force or fraud.

XIX.

What is the meaning of the word " law ?"
The will of the President.

XX.

How were the States formed ?
By the United States.

XXI.

Is the United States Government older than the States which made it ?
It is.

XXII.

Have the States any rights ?
None whatever, except when the President allows.

XXIII.

Have the people any rights ?
None but such as the President gives.

XXIV.

Who is the greatest martyr of history ?
John Brown.

XXV.

Who is the wisest man ?
Abraham Lincoln.

XXVI.

Who is Jeff. Davis ?
The devil.

LESSON THE SECOND.

I.

What is the "*habeas corpus*?"
The power of the President to imprison whom he pleases, as long as he pleases.

II.

What is Trial by Jury?
Trial by military commission.

III.

What is "security from unreasonable searches and seizures?" .
The liability of a man's house to be entered by any Provost Marshal who pleases.

IV.

What is the meaning of the promise that, "no person shall be held to answer for any crime unless on a presentment or indictment of a Grand Jury?"
That any person may be arrested whenever the President or any of his officers please.

V.

What is the meaning of the promise that, "no person shall be deprived of life, liberty or property, without due process of law?"
That any person may be deprived of life, liberty and property, whom the President orders to be so stripped.

VI.

What is the meaning of "the right to a speedy and public trial by an impartial jury?"

A remote secret inquisition conducted by a man's enemies.

VII.

What is the meaning of the promise that the accused shall be tried "in the State and district wherein the crime shall have been committed?"

That he shall be sent away from the State and beyond the jurisdiction of the district where the offenser is said to be committed.

VIII.

What is the meaning of the declaration that the accused shall "have the assistance of counsel fo his defense?"

That, in the language of Seward to the prisoners in Fort Warren, "the employment of counsel will be deemed new cause for imprisonment."

IX.

What is the meaning of the declaration that, "the right of the people to keep and bear arms shall not be infringed?"

That a man's house may be searched, and he be stripped of his arms, whenever and wherever a provost marshal dare attempt it.

X.

What is the meaning of the declaration that the accused shall be informed of the nature and cause of the accusation," against him ?

That he shall not be informed of the nature of his offence.

XI.

What is the meaning of the promise that an accused man may "be confronted with the witnesses against him ?"

That he shall not be allowed to confront them.

XII.

What is the meaning of the declaration that the accused "shall have compulsory process for obtaining witnesses in his favor ?"

That he shall not be allowed any witnesses.

XIII.

What is the meaning of the declaration that "the judicial Power of the United States shall be vested in the Supreme Court," etc. ?

That it shall be vested in the President and his provost marshals.

XIV.

What is the meaning of the declaration that "No bill of Attainder, or *ex post facto* law shall be passed ?"

That such a law may be passed whenever Congress pleases.

XV.

What is the meaning of the President's oath that he, "will to the best of his ability, Preserve, protect and defend the Constitution of the United States ?"

That he will do all in his power to subvert and destroy it.

XVI.

What is the meaning of that part of his oath in which he swears to " take care that the laws be faithfully executed " ?

That he will appoint provost marshals to override and disobey the laws.

XVII.

What is the meaning of the declaration that "The United States shall guarantee to every state a Republican form of government ?"

That Congress shall assist the President in destroying the Republican form of government in the States, and substituting a military government whenever he pleases—witness Missouri, Kentucky, Maryland, and Delaware.

XVIII.

What is the meaning of the declaration that " No attainder of Treason shall work corruption of blood, or forfeiture, except during the life of the person attainted ?

That a person accused of Treason may have his property confiscated not only during his life, but for all time, so that his children and heirs shall be punished for the crimes alleged against him.

XIX.

What is the meaning of the declaration, that " No person shall be convicted of treason unless on the testimony of two witnesses to some overt act, or on confession in open court?

That a man may be convicted of treason without any witness, and without judge or jury, and without having committed any overt act.

XX.

What is the meaning of the declaration that "No money shall be drawn from the Treasury but in consequence of appropriations made by law?"

That the President may draw money from the Treasury whenever he pleases, for such things as sending missionaries and teachers to teach contrabands to read and write, or to build sheds and houses for stolen or run-away negroes.

XXI.

What is the meaning of the government?
The President.

XXII.

What is the meaning of an oath?
To swear not to do the thing you promise.

XXIII.

What is truth?
A lie.

LESSON THE THIRD.

I.

Do loyal leaguers believe in the Ten Commandments?

They do.

II.

What are the Ten Commandments?

Thou shalt have no other God but the negro.

Thou shalt make an image of a negro, and place it on the Capitol as the type of the new American man.

Thou shalt swear that the negro shall be the equal of the white man.

Thou shalt fight thy battles on the Sabbath day, and thy generals, and thy captains, and thy privates, and thy servants, shall do all manner of murders, and thefts as on the other six days.

Thou shalt not honor nor obey thy father nor thy mother if they are Copperheads; but thou shalt serve, honor and obey Abraham Lincoln.

Thou shalt commit murder—of slaveholders.

Thou mayest commit adultery—with the contrabands.

Thou shalt steal—everything that belongeth to a slaveholder.

Thou shalt bear false witness—against all slaveholders.

Thou shalt covet the slave-holder's man-servant and his maid-servant, and shalt steal his ox and his ass, and everything that belongeth to him.

For on these commandments hang all the law and the honor of loyal leaguers.

III.

Do loyal leaguers believe the teachings of the gospel?

They do.

IV.

What does the gospel teach ?

That we shall hate those who believe not with us, and persecute those who never wronged us.

V.

What else does the gospel teach ?

That we shall resist evil, and that we shall overcome evil with evil.

VI.

What does the gospel say of peace-makers?

That they shall be accursed.

VII.

Whose children are the peace-makers ?

The children of the devil.

VIII.

Do Loyal Leagues believe in the Sermon on the Mount?

They do.

IX.

Repeat the Sermon on the Mount.

Blessed are the proud and the contractors, for theirs is the kingdom of greenbacks.

Blessed are they that do not mourn for them that are murdered in the abolition war, for they shall be comforted with office.

Blessed are the haughty, for they shall inherit shin-plasters.

Blessed are they that do hunger and thirst after the blood of slaveholders, for they shall be filled.

Blessed are the unmerciful, for they shall obtain command.

Blessed are the vile in heart, for they shall be appointed judges.

Whosoever does not smite thee on one cheek, smite him on both.

And if he turn away from thee, turn and hit him again.

If thou findest a chance to steal a slaveholder's coat, steal his cloak also.

Give to a negro that asketh not, but from the poor white man turn thou away.

Be ye therefore unkind, spiteful, and revengeful, even as your father the devil is the same.

Take heed that ye give alms in public to the negroes, otherwise ye have no reward of your father Abraham, who is in Washington.

Therefore when thou givest thine alms to a negro, do thou sound a trumpet before thee, as the ministers and hypocrites do in the churches and in the streets, that they may have glory of the contrabands.

And when thou doest alms let each hand know what the other hand doeth.

That thine alms may not be secret; and thy father the devil, who established the leagues, shall reward thee openly.

And when thou prayest, go to the Academy of Music, or to Cooper's Institute, that thou mayest be seen of men, after the manner of Cora Hatch and Henry Ward Beecher.

Do not forgive men their trespasses, for if you do God will not forgive your trespasses.

Moreover, when you pretend to fast, fast not at all, but eat turkies, ducks, and especially roosters, that ye may crow over the Copperheads, and stuff yourselves with whatsoever a shinplaster buyeth.

Lay up for yourselves treasures in greenbacks and five-twenties, and whatever else ye may steal from the Custom House and the Treasury.

Every man can serve two masters, the devil and the Abolitionists.

Take no thought to get raiment by honest toil, but go down South and steal it. Consider the vultures and the hawks, how they toil not neither do they sow, and yet no creature was ever stuffed out with so much fatness, except a contraband that feedeth at the public crib.

Judge another without judge or jury, but destroy the laws, so that your own measure shall not be measured unto you again.

If thou hast a beam in thine own eye, shut thine eye so that it cannot be seen, and go to picking out the mote that is in the Copperhead's eye.

If a poor white man ask bread, give him a stone, if he ask a fish, give him an alligator.

Therefore, whatsoever ye would that the slaveholder should not do unto you, do it even unto him: for this is the law of the loyal leagues.

X.

Have the loyal leagues a prayer?
They have.

XI.

Repeat it.
Father Abram, who art in Washington, of glorious

memory—since the date of thy proclamation to free negroes.

Thy kingdom come, and overthrow the republic; thy will be done, and the laws perish.

Give us this day our daily supply of greenbacks.

Forgive us our plunders, but destroy the Copperheads.

Lead us into fat pastures; but deliver us from the eye of detectives; and make us the equal of the negro; for such shall be our kingdom, and the glory of thy administration.

LESSON THE FOURTH.

I.

What is the motto of loyal leagues?
"Liberty to the slave, or death to the Union."

II.

Does this place the negro above the Union?
It does.

III.

What do loyal leagues call the masses of the people?
"A herd of cattle "—*vide* Secretary Stanton.

IV.

How many of this "Herd of cattle" have the abolitionists caused to be maimed or slain in this war?
One million.

V.

How many widows have they made?
Five hundred thousand.

VI.

How many orphans?
Ten hundred thousand.

VII.

What will Lincoln's administration cost the country?
Four thousand millions of dollars.

VIII.

What is the annual interest on this debt?
Two hundred and eighty millions of dollars.

IX.

How much will this interest amount to in ten years?
Two thousand and eight hundred million of dollars.

X.

How much will that be in twenty years?
Five thousand and six hundred million of dollars.

XI.

Would the entire surplus export production of the North pay the interest on its debt?
It would not.

XII.

How will this affect the people?
It will humble their pride, and make them feel that they have a government.

XIII.

What effect will this debt have on the farmer?
It will mortgage his farm to the Government for nearly the amount of the interest on its cash value.

XIV.

What effect will it have on the workingman?
It will mortgage his muscle and the sweat of his brow to the Government as long as he lives.

XV.

Is there any way for the people to get rid of this debt?

None whatever, but by repudiation.

XVI.

In case of repudiation, will " five twenties " go with the rest?

Yes—all government paper will sink together.

XVII.

How do the Republicans propose to prevent repudiation ?

By a standing army of *negroes*, to force the people to pay at the point of the bayonet.

XVIII.

Who must pay the expense of the standing army?

The people ; which will add three hundred millions annually to their debt.

XIX.

What will be the great advantage of this debt?

It will enslave the people, and bring them into the same wholesome subjection that they are in the Old World.

XX.

Is there any other benefit ?

Yes—It will enable the children of the rich to live, without industry, upon the earnings of the poor from generation to generation.

XXI.

Should Mr. Lincoln bo re-elected, what debt will
he leave upon the country at the end of his second
term ?

Eight billions, or *eight thousand millions* of dollars !

XII.

What will be the interest annually on this debt ?
Five hundred and sixty millions of dollars.

XIII.

What will be the annual expense for interest, and
the standing army ?

Eight hundred and sixty millions of dollars !

XIV.

Will it be possible for the people to stand such
a pressure of taxes ?

They will have to stand it, or stand the prick of the
bayonet.

XV.

Suppose the people should take it into their
heads to abandon their property and quit the country ?

They will not be allowed—but will be compelled to
remain and work for the support of the Government.

XVI.

Will this be just ?

Yes—" the government must be supported.'

LESSON THE FIFTH.

I.

What was Abraham Lincoln by trade?
A rail-splitter.

II

What is he now?
Union-splitter.

III.

Who is Sumner?
A free American of African descent, who would swear to support the Constitution " only as he understood it."

IV.

Who is Phillips?
One of the founders of the Republican party who " labored nineteen years to take fifteen states out of the Union."

V.

Who is Garrison?
A friend of the President, who went to hell, and found the original copy of the Constitution of the United States there.

VI.

Who is Seward?
A Prophet in the Temple of black dragons, and a taster in the government whiskey distillery.

VII.

Who is Chase?
The foreman of a green paper printing office.

VIII.

Who is Banks ?

A dancing master, who wanted to slide down hill with the Union.

IX.

Who is Wade ?

An amiable Christian gentlemen who wanted to " *wade* up to his knees in the blood of slaveholders."

X.

Who is Francis S. Spinner ?

A *spinner* of black yarn, who swore he would " abolish slavery, dissolve the Union, or have civil war," now Register of the Treasury.

XI.

Who is James S. Pike ?

A stale fish which Mr. Lincoln presented as a Minister to the Netherlands, because, he said, " The Union is not worth supporting in connection with the South."

XII.

Who is Judge Spaulding ?

A bad pot of *glue*, which would not hold the Union together, but declared in the Fremont Convention, "I am for dissolution, and I care not how soon it comes."

XIII.

Who is Jack Hale?

A hail fellow-well-met with the negroes, who introduced a petition to dissolve the Union in 1850.

XIV.

Who is Thomas F. Meagher ?

An absconding prisoner from Botany Bay, who came to New York to " squelch the Copperheads."

XV.

Who is Simeon Draper ?

A political *draper* by trade, who tried to *dress out* poor *Barney* of the Custom House, that he might make a *nice suit* for himself.

XVI.

Who is Horace Greeley?

A celebrated poet, who wrote a poem on the American Flag, beginning thus :

> "Tear down the flaunting lie!
> Half-mast the starry flag!
> Insult no sunny sky,
> With hate's polluted rag."

XVII.

Who is Owen Lovejoy ?

A fat and spongy Albino from Illinois. When it was supposed that his soul had floated off to Tartarus on the waves of his own fat ; a brother member of Congress kindly wrote his epitaph :

> Beneath this stone good Owen Lovejoy lies,
> Little in everything except in size ;
> What though his burly body fills this hole,
> Still through hell's key-hole crept his little soul.

And when good Owen returned to this mundane sphere, his arrival was celebrated by the following complimentary additional verse :

> The Devil finding Owen there,
> Began to flout and rave—and sware
> That hell should ne'er endure the stain,
> And kicked him back to earth again.

XVIII.

Who is Andrew Curtin?

A highly colored *screen*, to cover the whiskey in the Excutive Chamber of Pennsylvania.

XIX.

Who is John A. Dix?

A brave and invincible General, who never having had a chance to show prowess in battle, seized the Park Barracks containing seventy-five sick and wronged soldiers, and twenty-seven bushels of vermin.

XX.

Who is Park Godwin?

A celebrated Lexicographer, in the pay of Mr. Lincoln, who defines theft—"annoyance" and "botheration."

XXI.

Who is Henry J. Raymond?

A giant from the blood-stained plains of Solferino, enjoying a pension as Liar Extraordinary to the Administration.

XXII.

Who is the Rev. Henry Bellows?

A *windy instrument* of the abolitionists, who is trying very hard to make himself the equal of a negro.

XXIII.

Who is General Schenck?

A creature of very mixed *black and white* principles, which made an awful stink in Maryland.

XXIV.

Who is Thad Stephens?

An amalgamationist from Pennsylvania, who honestly practices what he preaches.

CATECHISM.

25

XXV.

Who is General Burnside?

A *fiery* commander who has had wonderful success in seizing peaceable and unarmed civilians, when they were asleep in their own beds at midnight; and who was once caught in a trap by a famous old trapper of the name of Lee.

XXVI.

Who is James T. Brady?

A gentleman of great political versatility, now affiliated with the amalgamationists, who believes that "A rose by any other name would smell as sweet."

XXVII.

Who is Anna Dickinson?

Ask Ben. Butler and William D. Kelly.

XXVIII.

Who is Ben. Butler?

A Satyr, who has the face of a devil and the heart of a beast, who laughed when Banks supplanted him in New Orleans, saying, "he will find it a squeezed lemon."

XXIX.

Who is William D. Kelly?

A member of Congress, and a wagon contractor, who plays a bass viol in the orchestra of the female loyal leagues.

XXX.

Who is Henry P. Stanton?

A white man, whose negro principles, are undergoing a bleaching process, in consequence of his having been made a scape-goat for all of Chase's forty thieves in the Custom House.

LESSON THE SIXTH.

I.

What is the chief end of the loyal leagues?
The end of the Union.

II.

What are States?
Colonies of the Federal Government.

III.

What is a Judge?
A provost marshal.

IV.

What is a court of law?
A body of soldiers, appointed by a General to try civilians without law.

V.

What is a Bastile?
A Republican meeting-house, for the involuntary assembling of men who believe in the Union as it was, and the Constitution as it is.

VI.

What is the meaning of the word "demagogue?"
Ask those members of Congress, who believe the war is for the negro, and for the destruction of the Union, and yet vote it supplies of men and money.

VII.

What is a Governor?
A general agent for the President.

VIII

What is a negro ?
A white man ith a black skin.

IX.

What is a white man ?
A negro with a white skin.

X.

What will be the effect of amalgamation?
It is the doctrine of the Leagues that a superior race will spring from amalgamation.

XI.

Is this according to science?
No,—science teaches that the progeny of amalgamation would run out, and become extinct after the fourth or fifth generation.

XII.

Is science true?
No—it must be a lie ; or the Leaguers are the greatest fools or knaves that ever lived.

XIII.

Is amalgamation now practiced to a greater extent than formerly ?
It is, to a much greater extent.

XIV.

Where?
Everywhere where Leagues prevail.

XV.

Is it prosperous in Washington ?

It is—so much so that more than five thousand of the fruits of amalgamation have been born in that city since the election of Mr. Lincoln.

XVI.

Is it spreading elsewhere ?

Yes—wherever the officers of our army go in the South, it is doing well.

XVII.

How is it in New Orleans ?

Well ;—but there are a great many squint-eyed yellow babies there, supposed to have been occasioned by fright at the presence of Ben. Butler.

XVIII.

Did the same thing occur at Fortress Monroe, after Ben. Butler was in command there ?

It did.

XIX.

The effects of fright are very wonderful in such cases, are they not ?

They are wonderful indeed.

XX.

Do such remarkable imitations ever spring from any other cause than fright ?

Yes—as in cases where such imitations follow good looking men, like Senators Wilson and Sumner.

XXI.

Is the science of amalgamation now in its infancy ?

Comparatively—but, under the patronage of the loyal leagues, a great number of practical and experimental works will soon be *issued*.

XXII.

Who are engaged on these works ?

The learned abolition clergy, Members of Congress, and all *competent* loyal leaguers.

XXIII.

Are the loyal leagues intended to be "*nurseries*" of the new science of amalgamation ?

They are.

XXIV.

Is amalgamation considered the true doctrine of *negro equality* as taught by Mr. Lincoln in his debates with Mr. Douglas?

It is.

XXV.

Is this what Anna Dickinson really means by " the lesson of the hour ?"

It is.

XXVI.

Is this what the President means by " Rising " with the occasion ?"

It is.

LESSON THE SEVENTH.

I.

Were the framers of the Constitution short-sighted and foolish men?

They were.

II.

Are their pernicious sentiments condemnatory of our most righteous abolition war?

They are.

III.

What did Jefferson, the father of the Declaration of Independence, teach?

That, " the several states which framed the Constitution have the unquestionable right to judge of infractions."

IV.

What did James Madison, the father of the Constitution, say?

That, "in case of a deliberate, palpable and dangerous exercise of powers not granted in the Compact, the States have a right to interfere, for maintaining within their respective limits the authorities, rights and liberties appertaining to them."

V.

What did John Quincy Adams say?

That, "if the day shall come—may Heaven avert it!—when the affections of the people of these States shall be alienated from each other, when this fraternal spirit shall give way to cold indifference, or collisions of interest shall fester into hatred—then the bands of political association will not hold together parties no longer attracted by the magnetism of conciliated interests and kindly sympathies, and far b ter will it be for the people of the disunited States part in friendship from each other than to be h together by restraint."

VI.

Have still later statesmen and politicians been affected with the same damnable idea?

They have.

VII.

What did Daniel Webster say?

" A bargain broken on one side is a bargain broken on all sides. "

VIII.

What did Andrew Jackson say in his farewell address?

That, "If such a struggle is once begun, and the citizens of one section of the country are arrayed in arms against those of the other, in doubtful conflict, let the battle result as it may, there will be an end of the Union, and with it an end of the hope of freedom. The victory of the injured would not secu to them the blessings of liberty ; it would aven their wrongs, but they would themselves share in t common ruin. The Constitution cannot be mai tained nor the Union preserved, in opposition to public feeling, by the mere exertion of the coercive powers confided to the government."

IX.

What did Abraham Lincoln say in Congress in 1848?

That, " Any people anywhere, being inclined, and having the power, have the RIGHT to rise up and shake off the existing government, and form a new one that suits them better. This is a most valuable a most sacred right—a right which we hope and believe, is to liberate the world. Nor is the right confined to the cause in which the whole people of an existing government may choose to exercise it. ANY PORTION of such people that CAN, MAY revolutionize and make their OWN of so much of the Territory as they inhabit. "

X.

What did Henry Clay say?

That, " When my State is right—when it has cause for resistance—when tyranny and wrong and oppression insufferable arise, I will share her fortunes. "

XI.

What did U. S. Senator Levi Woodbury of New Hampshire say?

That, " If the bonds of a common language, a common government and all the common glories of the last century, cannot make us conciliatory and kind—cannot make all sides forgive and forget something,—cannot persuade to some sacrifice even, if necessary, to hold us together, FORCE IS AS UNPROFITABLE TO ACCOMPLISH IT AS FRATRICIDE IS TO PERPETUATE PEACE IN A COMMON FAMILY."

XII.

What did Horace Greeley say in the *Tribune*, Nov. 26, 1860?

That, " If the Cotton States unitedly and earnestly wish to withdraw peacefully from the Union, we think they should be allowed to do so. Any attempt to compel them by force to remain, would be contrary to the principles enunciated in the immortal Declaration of independence."

XIII.

What did Mr. Greeley say in the *Tribune*, Dec. 17, 1860?

That, " We have repeatedly asked those who dissent from our view of this matter, to tell us frankly whether they do or do not assent to Mr. Jefferson's statement in the Declaration of Independence, that governments " derive their just powers from THE CONSENT OF THE GOVERNED ; and that, whenever any form of government becomes destructive of these ends, *it is the right of the people to alter or abolish it*, and to institute a new government, &c., &c. We do heartily accept this doctrine, believing it intrinsically *sound, beneficent,* and one that, universally accepted, is calculated to *prevent the shedding of seas of human blood.* AND, IF IT JUSTIFIED THE SECESSION FROM THE BRITISH EMPIRE OF THREE MILLIONS OF COLONISTS IN 1776, WE DO NOT SEE WHY IT WOULD NOT JUSTIFY THE SECESSION OF FIVE MILLIONS OF SOUTHERNERS FROM THE FEDERAL UNION in 1861. If we are mistaken on this point, why does not some one attempt to show wherein and why? For our own part, while we deny the right of slaveholders to hold slaves against the will of the latter, we cannot see how Twenty Millions of people can rightfully hold Ten or even Five Millions in a detested Union with them BY MILITARY FORCE."

If even "seven or eight States" send agents to Washington to say, "We want to get out of the Union," we shall feel constrained by our devotion to Human Liberty to say, *Let them go !* And we do not see how we could take the other side WITHOUT COMING IN DIRECT CONTACT WITH THOSE RIGHTS OF MAN WHICH WE HOLD PARAMOUNT TO ALL POLITICAL ARRANGEMENTS, however convenient and advantageous."

XIV.

What did Chancellor Walworth say March 1st 1861?

That, "It would be as brutal to send men to butcher their brothers of the Southern States, as it would be to massacre them in Northern States."

XV.

What did David S. Dickenson say in 1860?

That, "The Union is not to be maintained by force."

XVI.

What did Judge Amasa J. Parker say?

That, "our people shrink back aghast at the idea of repeating, in this enlightened age, that first great crime of man, the staining of their hands with a brother's blood."

XVII.

What did Senator Stephen A. Douglas say:

That, "I don't understand how a man can claim to be a friend of the Union, and yet be in favor of war upon ten millions of people in the Union. You cannot cover this up much longer under the pretext of love for the Union."

XVIII.

What did the address of the Democratic Sta Convention of New York say in 1861?

That "the worst and most ineffective argume that can be addressed by the Federal Government, or its adhering members, to the seceding States, is civil war. Civil war will not restore the Union, but will defeat forever its reconstruction."

XIX.

What did the Tammany Hall resolutions of March 1st, 1861, say?

That, "No State shall be coerced into remaining in this Union, when, in the judgment of her people, her safety requires that she should secede in order to protect the lives and property of her citizens.

"We will oppose any attempt on the part of the Republicans in power to make any armed aggression under the plea of 'enforcing the laws,' or 'preserving the Union,' upon the Southern States."

XX.

Are not the sentiments expressed by all the above named statesmen and politicians, the same as now held by such infamous traitors as Clement Vallandigham and C. Chauncey Burr?

They are.

XXI.

What ought to be done with such men as V landigham and Burr, who "cling to these dogm_ of the dead past?"

They ought to be hanged.

XXII.

Were Gen. Jackson and John Quincy Adams to come on earth again and teach the same as they once did, would they deserve to be hanged?

They would.

XXIII.

What should be done to Tammany Hall if it held the same doctrine now that it did three years ago?

It should be hanged, individually and collectively.

XXIV.

What should be done to Abraham Lincoln if he believed now as he did in 1818?

The king can do no wrong.

XXV.

Are all who believe as our fathers taught, "traitors' and " sympathizers ?'

They are.

XXVI.

What will become of all who believe in the Union as it was, and the Constitution as it is?

They shall be damned.

XXVII.

What shall be the reward of all such as believe the Union was a covenant with death, and the Constitution a compact with hell?

They shall be received into a negro Paradise.

LESSON THE NINTH.

I.

Is the United States a consolidated government?
It is.

II.

Who consolidated it?
Abraham Lincoln.

III.

Does consolidation mean to annihilate the States?
Yes—to a great extent.

IV.

Had he a right to do this?
Yes—under the war power.

V.

Who invented the war power?
Abraham Lincoln.

VI.

For what purpose did he invent the war power?
That he might not have to return to the business of splitting rails.

VII.

Was Mr. Lincoln ever distinguished as a military officer?
He was—In the Black Hawk war.

VIII.

What high military position did he hold in that war?
He was a cook.

IX.

Was he distinguished for anything except for his genius as a cook?

Yes—he often pretended to see Indians in the woods, where it was afterwards proved that none existed.

X.

Was he ever in any battle?

No—he prudently skedaddled, and went home at the approach of the first engagement.

XI.

Is there proof of this?

Yes—there are several men still living in Sangamon County, Illinois, who were present in the brigade at the time.

XII.

Does the Republican party intend to change the name of the United States?

It does.

XIII.

What do they intend to call it?

New Africa.

XIV.

How will New Africa be bordered?

On the North by the North Star, on the East by Boston, on the West by Sunset, and on the South by Salt-river.

XV.

Are the people of the United States happy?

They are, very.

XVI.

What do they live upon ?
Chiefly on blood.

XVII.

What do the Republicans understand by the word people ?
Abolitionists, mesmerisers, spiritual mediums, free-lovers and negroes.

XVIII.

What is to be the established religion of New Africa ?
Infidelity.

XIX.

How are the people to be divided?
Into the rich, the poor, the wise and the foolish.

XX.

Who are the rich ?
The Generals, the office-holders, and the thieves.

XXI.

Who are the poor ?
The soldiers, and all the people who are neither office-holders or thieves.

XXII.

Who are the wise ?
The Copperheads, because they are 'serpents.'

XXIII.

Who are the foolish ?
The black-snakes, because they are fast wriggling into a spot where they will run against the fangs of the Copperheads.

XXIV.

Is the black-snake afraid of the Copperheads?
Yes—as he is of the devil.

XXV.

What is the uniform of a chaplain of the leagues?
A shirt, a revolver, and a dirk.

XXVI.

How was this found out?
By the discovery of a Reverend loyal leaguer in
full uniform in a lady's chamber, in Massachusetts.

XXVII.

When caught did he confess that every loyal
leaguer is pledged to be always armed with these im-
plements?
He did.

XXVIII.

Did ho make a clean breast of the secrets of the
order?
Yes, he made a good deal cleaner *breast* than *shirt*.

XXIX.

What did the lady leaguer say when this loyal
chaplain was found in her room?
She said her husband was a brute to come home
when he wasn't wanted.

XXX.

Are all husbands brutes who go home when the
loyal league brethren are visiting their wives?
They are, great brutes.

LESSON THE TENTH.

I.

Are the loyal leaguers taught to hate any man?
They are.

II.

Who is he?
George B. McClellan.

III.

Why are they taught to hate McClellan?

Because he wished to restore the Union as it was, and preserve the Constitution as our fathers made it

IV.

Why do the loyal leagues wish the Union as it was, and the Constitution as it is, destroyed?

Because in no other way can they destroy the property of the South, and make the negro the equal of the white man.

V.

Is this the object of the war?
It is.

VI.

For what other reason are the leagues taught to hate McClellan?

Because he refused to let the army under his command steal or destroy the private property of the Southern people.

VII.

Are these the reasons why he was removed from command?

They are—because his great popularity with the soldiers might render him a stumbling-block in the Presidential campaign for 1864.

VIII.

Has Mr. Lincoln any other stumbling-blocks?
He has.

IX.

Can you name them?

General Fremont is one, and Lincoln fears, a very dangerous one.

X.

Is this the reason Mr. Lincoln has not given him a command?
It is

XI.

Did Mr. Lincoln approve of the principles of Fremont's campaign in the West?

He did, approve of every thing except his aspirations for the presidency, and his popularity anong the Germans.

XII.

What other stumbling-block has Mr. Lincoln?

Chase, who is trying to buy his own nomination, by putting extra steam on his high-pressure greenback printing machines.

XIII.

What is Mr. Seward in this contest?
A broken bubble.

XIV.

When does Seward think the war will end?
In sixty days.

XV.

When does Lincoln expect it will end?
When Afric's woods are moved to Washington.

XVI.

Who is Mrs. Lincoln?
The wife of the government.

XVII.

Who is Mr. Lincoln?
A successful contractor to supply the government with mules.

XVIII.

Who is Master Bob Lincoln?
A lucky boy, yet in his teens, who has been so happy as to obtain shares in Government Contracts by which he has realized $300,000.

LESSON THE ELEVENTH.

I.

What is the meaning of the word swamp?

It is a place in Florida where Mr. Lincoln proposes to hide a small number of Yankees, to act as presidential electors for him next fall.

II.

What is a lagoon?

A place in Louisiana to be used for the same purpose.

III.

What is the meaning of the phrase to count chickens before they are hatched?

Mr. Lincoln's reckoning upon the quiet submission of all the states to his scheme of electoral frauds.

IV.

What does he fear?

That, when the pinch comes at last, the people will fly to arms and make an end of his rotten borough system and of himself together.

V.

What is a bank-director?

A silly coon, caught in one of Chase's traps.

VI.

What is a government bank?

A new engine turned loose on the track to run over all the State banks.

VII.

What will be the result?

That all banks, State and National, will be smashed up together.

VIII.

What are Five-Twenties?

Lincoln *I. O. U's.*—made redeemable in government slips of paper, in five or twenty years.

IX.

What else are they?

Baits to catch *flat* fish.

X.

Are loyal leaguers allowed to refer to the Constitution?

Only in terms of reproach.

XI.

Is it a disloyal practice to refer to the exploded right of trial by jury?

It is very disloyal.

XII.

Is it disloyal to refer to the size of Old Abe's feet?

It is.

XIII.

Is it disloyal to speak of white men as a superior race?

It is, very.

XIV.

Is it disloyal for a husband to object to his house being visited by strange men whose acquaintance his wife forms at the meetings of the loyal leagues?

It is, shockingly disloyal.

XV.

Is it disloyal to believe in the Union as it was ?
It is.

XVI.

Is it a disloyal practice to say that the abolitionists
ought to do the fighting in their war for the negroes?
It is, dangerously disloyal.

XVII.

Is it disloyal to allude to the rate at which the Republicans are plundering the Treasury and the people?
It is.

XVIII.

Is it disloyal to allude to the difference between an
old fashioned Democratic gold dollar and the Republican green paper dollars?
It is.

XIX.

Is it disloyal to allude to the opinions and practices
of our fathers on civil liberty or the rights of the
States?
It is.

XX.

Is it disloyal for a man to sympathze with the family of a murdered friend or relative in the South?
It is, wickedly disloyal.

XXI.

Is it disloyal to honestly believe in one's heart that
if Lincoln is not a fool he is a knave, and that if he
is not a knave he is a fool?
It is, horribly disloyal.

www.ingramcontent.com/pod-product-compliance
Lightning Source LLC
Chambersburg PA
CBHW021558270326

41931CB00009B/1283